Contents

Isaac Oliver miniature, 1617

Here are two photographs taken last year.
These children go to school like you.
Their toys and clothes are the same as yours.

Here is a wedding thirty
years ago.

The two bridesmaids are
sisters.
They were five and nine
years old.

Today they are both mums.

William Brown St., Liverpool, 1900

Here are some boys sitting by a fountain.
Look carefully at their clothes.
They are wearing caps, suits and boots.
Not one of them wears glasses.

Did they take their boots off to
paddle in the fountain?

The children in this photograph are wearing their best clothes.

They look solemn because they had to stand very still for the camera.

The boys are wearing sailor suits.

c. 1888

Two children have hats and laced boots.

All these children were alive about a hundred years ago.

These children are dressed up in clothes made a hundred years ago.

The little boy has a toy horse on wheels.
He pulls it with a string.

A hundred years ago little girls were made to
sit still on chairs. They were told to look pretty.

Pictures were drawn before
cameras were invented.
Find the little girl in the
big cotton factory.

She worked at a huge machine.

She had no shoes to wear.

The girl's brother worked too.
He was small and climbed inside big chimneys.
Look at all the rods he used to make the big brush longer.
The soot from the coal fires made him very dirty.

Some children even had to
work carrying coal from
under the ground.

Family of George III (detail) by Johan Zoffany, c. 1771

Here are four royal children.
They lived at the same time as
the children at work.

Their father was King George III
and an artist painted their picture.

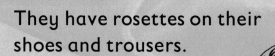

Look how different their clothes
are from the factory girl, the
miners and the chimney sweep.

Their clothes are made of
velvet, silk, satin and lace.

They have rosettes on their
shoes and trousers.

What animals can you see
in the picture with them?

Boy or girl?

Portrait of a Little Boy by George Romney

Little boys were dressed the same as girls until they were eight or nine, so this is a painting of a little boy.

He wore a skirt and a cap with a bow.

What is he doing with his satin belt?

Sir John Thynne's daughter, 20 months, by Hans Eworth 1672

This little girl wore a cap, collar and apron.
She carried a rattle and cherries.

What is she wearing round her neck?

The girl lived sixty years earlier than the boy.

Charles I, by Robert Peake The Elder

Four hundred years ago
Prince Charles, Duke of York,
was dressed up for this painting.

He wore an embroidered dress
with a lace collar.

But a prince had to look brave.
Look under the collar.
He wears a piece of armour
like soldiers used to wear.

He has a sword and a lance too.

Prince Charles' baby sister died.

Here is her grave, with a
picture of her carved in stone.

Westminster Abbey, 1606

These very small pictures are called miniatures.
They were sometimes worn as brooches.

Look at them closely.

Isaac Oliver miniatures, 1617

One girl was four years old.   Her sister was five.

Would you like to wear clothes like theirs?

Here is another royal prince.
He was eight years of age,
old enough to wear trousers,
a fancy cap and a ruff around his neck.

The falcon on his wrist was
for hunting birds.

James I, (1566–1625) by Rowland Lockey

Families four hundred years ago

Here is the Cobham family at a meal.
They are going to eat some fruit.

Baron Cobham and his family, by the Master of the Countess of Warwick, 156...

How many children are there?
They were aged two, one, six and four.
Look for the twins. They were five.
Their mother is on the left.

A pet bird has hopped onto the table.

This picture of brothers and sisters was cut in brass.
It is part of their parents' grave in a church.

Francis Holbrooke's children, from Newington near Sittingbourne, Kent, 1581

The children are dressed like the Cobham
family and lived at the same time.
How many children are there?

Four hundred years ago mothers sometimes
had as many as six children, but babies often died.

Here are some schoolboys who lived
more than five hundred years ago.

Can you see their books?
One boy is being beaten by the teacher.

Misericord, St. Botolph, Boston, Lincs.

This picture was carved underneath
a seat in a church.

The seat is made of wood.

This is a really ancient picture.

The schoolboys are ancient Romans.
They are wearing loose clothes and sandals.

The picture has lasted two thousand years
because it was cut in stone.

Now look again at some of the children in the past. Which one would you like to have been?

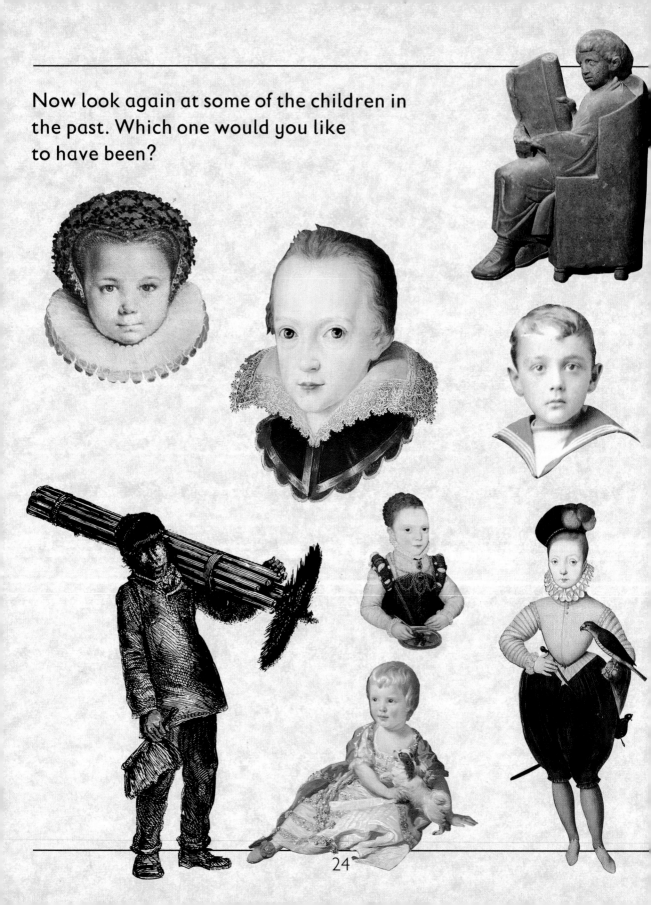